GUN SHY

ANGIE MCDONNELL

Published by Accent Press Ltd 2017

ISBN 9781786155474

The Quick Reads project in Wales is an initiative coordinated by the Welsh Books Council and supported by the Welsh Government.

Chapter One

The New Boy in Camp

"Have you seen the new boy in town?" Tash teased.

I shook my head and looked up from the medical kit I was preparing.

"Flew in on the helicopter from Camp Bastion yesterday. He was walking down by the gym when I saw him," she continued.

"Just my luck to miss out. What's he like?"

"You'll love him, Angie. He's different to the others - looks well fierce."

"I bet underneath he's just as soppy as the rest of them," I said, hoping that soon I would catch up with this new protector in our camp.

Tash and I had been in Afghanistan for two months and had become good friends. We were on Operation Herrick, the British Army's codename for all combat operations in this war. As combat medics we were helping to take care of troops wounded on the front line in the fight against the Taliban.

The British and American Armies had been

at war with the Taliban since the 9/11 terrorist attacks on the United States in 2001. The terrorist group al-Qaeda, led by Osama bin Laden, had their training camps in Afghanistan and the allied forces were fighting to drive them out, end the Taliban's reign of terror over the people of Afghanistan and return the country to peace. By the time we arrived more than 400 British soldiers had been killed and countless others injured. So the doctors, nurses, paramedics and health care assistants of the Army Medical Corps were much needed.

Our base at Lashkar Gah Durai was in the east of Helmand province and was densely planted with landmines and explosives. As the centre of the world's opium drug trade, the fields and countryside of Helmand were thick with poppies. This made it an area that the Taliban was keen to control and willing to shed blood over. In the six years since the war in Afghanistan had begun, Helmand had been the scene of some of the fiercest fighting. It had 9,500 troops stationed there at the height of the conflict and 137 military stations dotted around the vast area of arid and dry countryside.

Camp Lash Durai, as the troops on the ground called it, was the patrol base for the

British Army's headquarters at Lashkar Gah, so there was never a dull moment. Set beside Highway 1, the main road running through Afghanistan, it was vital for the allied forces in their mission to maintain control of the area. There was the constant drone of the Warrior Armoured Fighting Vehicles (AFVs) as they left for patrols and the "whacker, whacker, whacker" sound of the helicopters as they arrived with their cargos of troops, supplies and equipment, whipping up a storm of dry, orange 'moon dust' from the desert over everything. No-one travelled by road unless they were out on operations. It was too dangerous. Many soldiers had lost limbs and even their lives to bombs planted beneath the sands and hard dirt roads of the desert, so helicopters were the way to get around.

Adding to the sound level was the noise of the Afghan National Police, who had their own compound opposite ours, and the chaotic din from the car horns of Afghan locals trying to go about their business. Often, you would hear the bang of explosives and gunshots echoing in the distance.

Lash Durai was a 'transient camp', meaning no-one stayed for too long. It was the furthest point east from the Army's main base at Camp Bastion and acted as a stopping-off point to other camps in the area. As a result, there was a stream of American and British soldiers passing through on their way to and from operations in the desert. For some it was also the last stop before making the twenty-minute helicopter ride to Bastion – and then home.

Tash was twenty and a full-time soldier and combat medical technician with the 3 Medical Regiment and I was a Reserve Medic. I had taken leave from my full-time job as a paramedic to follow my dream to become a soldier. We had left behind our families and friends to join the British Army in the desert in one of the bloodiest battles since World War Two. There were few women stationed at our camp, so Tash and I had formed a close bond. 'Tour Mum', Tash called me, and at twice her age, my instinct was to protect her.

***

That afternoon I was out on a run around the camp, as we were expected to keep our fitness levels up when we weren't working. Quite often I would run a couple of circuits around the inside of the perimeter fence. I passed the gym and carried on running until I came to the kennels, hoping to find a Springer spaniel in need of a cuddle after a busy day sniffing out enemy explosives. But the cages were empty, so I turned and headed for the track past the living quarters, where T-shirts and khakis were hanging off the tent ropes, drying in the fifty-degree heat.

And that's when I saw him.

He was part of the team whose job was to find and safely detonate roadside bombs – or Improvised Explosive Devices (IEDs) as the military called them. Hidden in the ground around the villages and surrounding fields, these bombs were planted by Taliban fighters and lay in wait to blow to pieces anyone, or anything, that touched them.

Tash was right, he did look fierce. I took a detour in his direction to get closer. He was sitting upright, ears pricked, nose in the air. Aloof or alert, I wondered. As I moved nearer I noticed a massive fly dancing across his big, black muzzle. But he didn't move, just sat there waiting for the next command.

Suddenly a voice shouted: "Don't touch the dog." His handler was warning me off.

"Is he a German shepherd?" I asked.

Immediately I thought back to my childhood and the day I had come home from school to find my mum, dad and older sister standing in the kitchen looking out into the garden. A German shepherd dog had been abandoned by a neighbour in our back yard.

With the excitement and total lack of awareness that only an eight-year-old possesses, I ran out into the garden and threw my arms around the dog's neck. As my parents held their breath, fearing for my safety, the dog melted into my arms. In that moment Bess and I became the best of friends. She made herself at home in our house and that was it. We played ball together, I took her for walks and I would sit next to her in her basket, hugging her and blowing raspberries on her nose. She may have been thirty kilos of pure muscle with the look of a guard dog that could rip your arm off if you got on her wrong side, but she was a softy. Her rightful owner never reclaimed her so Bess and I remained best mates for many years, until her back legs started to give way on her. The vet said she had severe hip dysplasia, a common problem with large breeds like German shepherds. Bess was too old to undergo an operation. Having to decide whether to put your best friend out of her misery is a choice no thirteen-year-old should have to make.

"Close. He's a Mallie," the handler said, bringing me back to the present.

He was certainly strong and handsome like a German shepherd. Being a Belgian Malinois, he had big black erect ears and a powerful muzzle. His coat was light brown, flecked with black, and with a solid black line running down his spine. He had a matching black snout, which made him look like he was wearing a Batman mask. Looking more closely I could see he was slightly smaller than a German shepherd, with shorter fur. But he had the same sad look in his deep brown eyes that Bess had on the day I said goodbye to her.

"What's his name?" I asked.

"Vidar," his handler replied.

"Vidar. Vidar. Vidar," I called.

Nothing. He sat tight against his handler's leg, his doleful chocolate eyes fixed in the distance. He completely ignored me. I wasn't used to the working dogs on camp being so unfriendly. The spaniels with their waggy bottoms were always up for a game of frisbee or a head rub. And the off-duty Labradors spent half their time on their backs waiting for a tummy tickle. But this dog was playing hard to get.

I made it my mission to win Vidar's trust.

***

From then on, I made a point of looking out for Vidar and his handler Tom whenever I was out on my runs. Tom would tell me where they had been on patrol and all about what Vidar had sniffed out that day. Tom was

Vidar's fourth handler in his career as a Military Working Dog and although their partnership was still quite new, they made an effective team.

During my conversations with Tom I discovered why Mallies were so popular as working Army dogs. They got their name from the Belgian town of Malines, where they were first bred for herding and guarding sheep. Purposeful, intelligent, they are fast on their feet and quick to learn and make excellent sniffer and guard dogs. It was a common belief that a Mallie led the raid on Osama bin Laden's hideout.

The more I saw them, the more Vidar trusted me, and I soon got to know the gentle soul under the tough exterior. Sometimes I would volunteer to take him for walks around the camp, as Mallies can never get enough exercise. Other times I would play with his rope tug toy – he loved a game of tug-o-war and usually won. And at night I would often slip out to the kennels, before going to bed, to check on him and kiss him goodnight.

One night I was lying in my cot bed at the back of the medical centre, when I was woken by a loud noise. There was a hail of gunfire in the distance and the loud explosion of what sounded like grenades whistling across the sky.

I thought of the dogs and ran down to the kennel to check on Vidar. As I peered through the bars of the cage, I could just make out the outline of a dog, curled into a ball, tucked away in the back of the run, trembling. Hearing the gate open, he lifted his head up. In the darkness, I could see the whites of his eyes.

Boom! Another bomb erupted in the distance and Vidar dropped his head low and tucked his tail tight under his body.

"It's OK, Vidar," I said as I knelt in the kennel beside him. I ran my hand down his back and could feel him shivering. I felt his weight leaning against my body as I cuddled him closer. "You're safe here, I won't let anything hurt you."

Poor Vidar. For a big brave Army dog, he was petrified.

Chapter Two

A Military Dog in the Making

In my talks with Tom, I learnt a lot about military dogs and their training.

From the day he was born, Vidar was destined to be a dog of war. He had started his puppy life in the Bosnian capital, Sarajevo, where he was handpicked to be trained at one of the world's best-known training centres for mine-clearance dogs, the Norwegian People's Aid Global Training Centre. His dad had been a military sniffer dog working in the war zones of Bosnia and Herzegovina and had fathered almost sixty top-notch working dogs. His mother was also a mine and explosives detection dog. Two of his sisters, Viske and Vroom (all the pups from his litter had names starting with the letter V), were also trained as Army detection dogs. So Vidar was following in a family tradition.

Only the strongest, most resilient and sociable dogs made the grade. As Vidar grew from a tiny bundle of beige fluff into solid

Mallie muscle, his Norwegian trainers drilled into him the basic commands that would prepare him for a life in service. It's one thing teaching a cute pet puppy to roll over and give paw, but these puppies needed to be ultra-obedient. He was taught commands in Norwegian such as "kom" for come, "foot" for heel and "lig" for lie down. He was also taught to remain quiet and not bark – an important command when he would be leading troops out on dangerous war operations. He was taught to pick up the smell of explosives buried more than six metres below the ground and sniff out bombs that had been hidden for decades.

Once he'd passed his assessments and proved he was strong enough to work in difficult conditions, he'd been sent to the British Army's Defence Animal Centre training centre near Melton Mowbray. There he joined 400 or so other military dogs, dogs which have played an important role in every war from World War One right through to the conflicts in Northern Ireland, Bosnia, Iraq and Afghanistan. With a sense of smell 1000 times more effective than a human's, they can lead front line patrols and alert commanders to an enemy attack from more than 1000 metres away. They stand guard at Army bases, protecting the soldiers within. They search vehicles for weapons, bombs and bullets at check points. In many cases a dog can do the job of two or three soldiers.

Their regimental motto is 'Vires in Varietate', which means 'Strength in Diversity', and the different breeds play to their strengths. The German shepherds and Mallies – each with forty-two ferociously sharp teeth – make excellent guard dogs. I know who I'd take my chances with if I was faced with a soldier and a Mallie! The bouncy Springer and Cocker spaniels are at their best when leaping into vehicles and slinking into tight spaces searching for arms, explosives and drugs. What the Labrador retrievers lack in ferocity, with their cute Andrex-puppy looks, they make up for in the detection stakes making them great all-round search dogs.

Vidar worked hard and when he was two years old was teamed up with his first handler, Luke, who was a young private with the Royal Army Veterinary Corps. It was Luke's first time as a search dog handler and it was Vidar's first call-up as an IED search dog, so they made a perfect pair.

In Afghanistan there was an unwritten rule that the dogs protect the troops in the heat of war, and the handlers look after them in the heat of the desert. So the bond between Vidar and his handler first took shape during their six months' training with a Military Working Dog regiment in Germany and then in the arid sand dunes of Jordan, where they both got a sense of what it would be like working in Afghanistan. For Vidar it was a chance to put his highly trained sense of smell into practice as he was ordered to sniff out explosives and pressure plates buried underground. These were inactive but there would be real dangers in Afghanistan, where he would be sent in when it was too perilous for foot soldiers with metal detectors.

It was essential that the pair could work as one and that meant Luke being able to read Vidar's body language and watch how he worked, so that when Vidar picked up the scent of live explosives he could call for expert back-up. Many of the bravest, cleverest and best trained soldiers had been blown apart stepping onto landmines. Search dogs like Vidar were vital to maintain safe routes for foot patrols and the local villagers.

Vidar was a happy Mallie. When he first arrived at the Kalang patrol base in Afghanistan he was almost two and a half years old, which in dog years meant he was still a teenager. He was young, handsome and boisterous. He worked hard and wanted to play hard too. He was good at his job and knew it and made sure everyone else on camp knew it too.

He made lots of friends among the sappers of the Royal Engineers, who they worked alongside. After a physically exhausting patrol duty clearing IEDs, having a mischievous and playful dog around lifted spirits in camp. It was hard to be miserable when Vidar was demanding the boys threw a ball for him or tickled his belly. When he was off duty, his favourite position was on his back, legs in the air, showing off his bits as if to say, "Look at me, boys". It took the men's minds off the harsh and hazardous jobs that lay ahead, and boosted morale. Often to keep Vidar entertained and active, Luke would lay bits of copper wire around the compound so he could practise his search skills. But it didn't take him long to get wise and know the hiding places.

Wherever Luke was, Vidar was never far away. As a dog handler, Luke had the responsibility for looking after his dog as well as his own safety and that of the soldiers he was working with. He was trained in doggy first aid and carried a vet kit at all times. It included bandages, tweezers to remove splinters or shrapnel from paw pads, gels to flush out germs from cuts and grazes and glucose gels to add to Vidar's water when his energy was draining in the heat. He even knew how to give Vidar the canine kiss-of-life in an emergency.

Out on operations Luke carried the extra weight of supplies for Vidar with enough dried food to last forty-eight hours in case they were stranded, water to stop him dehydrating in the intense heat and a toy to reward him for a job well done. On top of that there was Vidar's protection kit – a bullet-proof vest, boots, earmuffs and 'doggles' to protect his eyes from sand whipped up by the wind and helicopter downdrafts. The rubberised boots, designed to protect paws on rough and sharp terrain, didn't go down well with Vidar. When Luke tried to fasten the Velcro straps around his paws, he looked at him as if to say, "What the hell are these?" and walked around like a dandy, before kicking them off and chewing them. Any protection the earmuffs might have provided against loud bangs and explosions was equally lost on Vidar. The more docile breeds like spaniels and Labradors would happily walk around in them as if they were sporting a pair of Beats by Dr Dre headphones. Not him. He'd rub his head on the ground until they fell off.

Even at bedtimes they were a close couple. Camel spiders are famous in Afghanistan. The sandy-coloured predators look like a cross between a tarantula and a scorpion. At six inches long, they can kill animals three or four times their size and eat them using their powerful jaws to turn their victims into pulp. Their jaws can also give humans a nasty bite and camps were rife with tales of close shaves with these creatures. So when Luke spotted one in the area around their sleeping tent, he took action and moved Vidar from the makeshift outdoor kennel where he usually bedded down to a place under his bed where they could both be protected by a mosquito net. Knowing Vidar's playfulness and curiosity he might easily have eaten one or been bitten. It was another example of Luke's concern for Vidar's safety, even if it meant being woken up by Vidar's snoring.

Chapter Three
Fight or Flight?

During one of our many chats, Tom told me how worries about Vidar's behaviour were first highlighted when he was working with Luke at the Loy Mandeh Bazaar. The bazaar had been a bustling marketplace, where Afghan farmers traded fruit, vegetables and spices, and locals bartered for ornate clothes and silver jewellery. That was, until the Taliban moved in. After a bomb exploded, killing and injuring dozens of people, the locals had deserted the area fearing for their lives and livelihoods.

Now it was a ghost town. Sandy stone pillars that had once marked the entrance to this thriving centre of business lay broken and crumbling on the dusty ground. Shops had been reduced to rubble, the tangled steel shutters no longer able to protect the goods within. It bore all the marks of the brutal battles between allied forces and the enemy for control.

Four Royal Marines had already lost their lives in the fight to drive the Taliban out. But the enemy was not prepared to give up. They had booby-trapped the area with hundreds of IEDs hidden in the ground waiting to kill anyone who came back.

Into this powder keg of danger, Vidar and Luke were dispatched.

They were working with Royal Engineers who had the job of clearing the roads and alleyways around the bazaar of metal, ropes and wires left over from the battles. Local governors and traders in the area were desperate to move back in and rebuild their lives but the Army had to make sure that it was safe.

Vidar shook the dust from his coat and set off on command. Tail in the air, nose to the ground, he paced the earthy roadway, searching for the tell-tale scent of explosives.

Seconds later he stopped. To the soldiers and their lieutenant who were waiting at a safe distance, there was no obvious sign of an IED at the spot where Vidar was sniffing. But Vidar's highly trained nose told a different story. His sudden change in behaviour was a sure-fire indication to Luke that there was something deadly in the ground. To the untrained eye the fact that Vidar had moved his body in a different way meant nothing, but Luke knew he had sensed explosives. It might be a pressure plate, a wire or a battery pack connected to a deadly explosive charge waiting to detonate. Job done, he called Vidar to heel.

"Get your kit and move back," the lieutenant commanded. As the troops withdrew over the bridge to safety, Vidar returned to his handler's side.

Carefully, an explosives expert inspected the area where Vidar's nose had stopped and found a suspicious wire, which led to a pressure plate. If one of the soldiers had stepped on it, it was likely they would have been torn apart.

"One minute to controlled detonation. Everybody down!" the lieutenant shouted.

"Ten, nine, eight..." the countdown began. As the troops ducked for cover, Vidar started to shake.

Ears pinned back, showing the whites of his eyes, Vidar started quivering and licking his lips, a sign that Luke knew all too well meant he was uneasy. It did not look like the reaction of a proud hero dog whose super-sensitive nose had potentially saved another life.

"Three, two, one." Boom! The ground tore open, spewing jagged metal, red-hot dust and rocks across the road.

"What's up with Vidar?" one of the engineers asked Luke, who was holding onto Vidar's collar as he cowered.

"I think he's gun shy," Luke explained. "He's never been comfortable with explosions. But he seems to be getting worse. It doesn't help that he's been hit by stones and rocks from an exploding bomb. Now as soon as he hears the countdown he just wants to run. Sometimes I have to pin him down under me when I take cover before explosions."

Vidar was definitely showing signs of stress. Whenever he heard loud explosions he would try to run away and, if he couldn't escape, he would tremble. It was getting worse and the recovery time between episodes was getting longer: some days he was too scared to carry on working. Concerned for his welfare, Luke reported back to his senior commanders in the Royal Army Veterinary Corps and Vidar was flown back to Camp Bastion for tests.

Even getting him back to Bastion was a trial for Vidar. He was petrified of the noise of helicopters, and that was the only way to travel. When the rotors were spinning, creating a downdraft, he dug his heels in and refused to run onto the aircraft. Luke had to pick him up and run on with him in his arms.

However, at Bastion, the animal behaviour specialists tested Vidar's reactions using firecrackers and grenades and deemed him fit for work. So he was sent back to Luke.

***

Returning to duty, they were deployed to join the task force on an operation to bring stability back to the area. In one village the Army was working with the elders and the Afghan National Army and police to work out what they needed to do to rebuild the area. This meeting, called a Shura, brought all parties together to build trust and create a plan for a safe and secure future.

But it was a volatile situation. Driven out, the Taliban saw the meetings as a threat to their control and there was a real danger they would attack. Inside the building, a group of Afghans with long beards and wrinkled faces pointed their bony fingers at the Army commanders, demanding action to make their village safe. Outside, the British infantry formed a protective ring around the meeting place. Vidar had his nose to the ground, sniffing for bombs in the buildings and ground around the Shura, while Luke maintained a safe distance from him on the other end of a fifteen-metre line.

Suddenly a fireball tore across the sky,

followed by a hail of machine-gun fire. The insurgents were on the attack. The infantry dived for cover and started to fight back. Bullets screamed over the village, mortar bombs landed, blasting craters on the ground. The village elders ran for safety.

When a rocket-propelled grenade erupted nearby, Vidar's fight or flight instinct kicked in and he ran for cover. As he ran, further and further away from the noise, his leash slipped out of Luke's hands and he was gone. Luke watched helplessly as the outline of his dog disappeared over the horizon – out of sight and out of earshot of the bangs.

He had to find him, but he could not break away from the unit to go looking for him. As the bullets and grenades rained down, Luke had an agonising wait. The battle raged on and when the firefight eventually ended, he was given the all-clear to go out into the wilderness and search for Vidar.

"Have you seen my dog?" he asked a group of infantry on the outskirts of the village.

"He went that way, ages ago. But you ain't gonna find him," one said, pointing his weapon in the direction Vidar had run.

"He's my dog. I've got to find him," Luke protested. A couple of willing soldiers joined him and they headed off. Vidar had an hour's head start on Luke, but they were a team. There was no way Luke was going to let him die in the desert, even if it meant putting his own life on the line.

Meanwhile the Afghan Army were listening in to the Taliban's radio signals. "If you see three soldiers on their own, kill them," came the order. Unaware, Luke and his colleagues kept searching.

Eventually Luke had to admit defeat and rejoined the rest of the troop as they withdrew back to patrol base. If he had lost one of his fellow soldiers, he could not have hurt more. The insurgents treated humans with brutality – he could only imagine what they would do to an animal. Dogs were for fighting and beating. His only hope was that Vidar would use his super-sensitive nose and pick up his scent back to camp.

When Luke and the rest of the unit returned to the patrol base at Kalang, he was greeted with the news that an Afghan Army commander had found a dog tied up in a village three miles away. It was waiting in the kennels. Luke rushed down to see if it was his dog.

There, huddled at the back of the kennel, head hung low, sat Vidar. When he heard Luke's footsteps, he stood up, eyes cast down to the floor as if to say, "Sorry I let you down, Dad, but I was frightened."

"What's happened to you, boy? You scared me to death," Luke whispered as he topped up a bowl of water for him and gave him food.

He had been missing for five hours and there was no way of knowing what had happened to him in that time. The Taliban thought all dogs were dirty and they were either treated with disdain and left tied up and starving or, if they were fit and strong like Vidar, they would bait them in dog fights.

Vidar had no physical scars to show for his ordeal, but mentally he was not the same dog. He had lost the cheeky glint in his eye and the playful wag to his tail.

It was after this experience that Luke put the words 'Gun Shy' on Vidar's military notes. Luke returned home to the UK but Vidar stayed out in Bastion and worked with two other handlers before he was finally paired up with Tom.

So that was Vidar's life before I met him. But what of my early life...?

Chapter Four
From Ambulances to Army

As a little girl there were two things I really loved: my dog and the Army. Growing up in London in the eighties I would nag my dad to take me to the Royal Tournament at Earl's Court. In those days it was the place to be if you wanted to see the might of the British military in action.

Teams from the Royal Navy, Army and Air Force would show off their skills in competitions. The pomp and ceremony of soldiers parading in their perfectly turned-out uniforms; the sounds of the marching bands; the thundering hooves of the horses and mounted soldiers of the Household Cavalry. I couldn't get enough of it.

My granddad and great-granddad had both fought in World War Two. Granddad Bill had been a soldier in North Africa while Great-granddad George, a rear gunner in the Royal Air Force, was awarded the Burma Star for his service in Asia. They never spoke about the horror they witnessed on the front line. But after Granddad Bill passed away I was looking through his old photographs and found an image of hundreds of bodies piled in a shallow grave. Whether they were his friends or enemies, I would never know. He had taken those horrific memories with him to the grave. I was proud that this quiet man had fought for our freedom and I wanted to follow in his footsteps.

Leaving school at sixteen with no qualifications, I headed down to the local Army recruitment office to follow my Army dream. But after sitting the initial tests and medical examinations, I was rejected because I had asthma. This was news to me as I had never had any problems with my chest or breathing, but I was told it ruled out a military career. I was gutted. So I drifted from job to job, never sticking to anything for longer than a couple of months. Then at twenty-two I got a job as an ambulance driver ferrying elderly patients to hospital appointments, clinics and day centres. It wasn't exactly defending the country, but at least I was helping others.

At twenty-four I joined the emergency services as a trainee technician with London Ambulance working in the Brixton and

Clapham areas of south London. I was trained to save the lives of heart attack patients and deal with people who had suffered terrible spine and head injuries in accidents. I learnt how to stop bleeding and treat the wounds and broken bones of patients injured in accidents. Over the years I worked my way up to become a paramedic.

In many ways it was like being on the front line. Whenever there was a call-out, I never knew what I was going to see when our blue lights arrived on the scene. A shopper collapsed in the middle of a busy street? A multiple car crash? A pensioner who had fallen downstairs? A street attack? A young woman beaten by her violent partner at home? In fact, I saw more bullet wounds on the streets of Brixton than I ever did out in Afghanistan.

Over the years I witnessed some traumatic scenes: a young girl who had hanged herself with the electric cord of a kitchen blender; an elderly man who had slept next to the body of his dead wife because he couldn't bear to be parted from her. Yet there were also happy times when I would be called on to help a new mum deliver a beautiful baby, or I would arrive at the scene of a freak accident and help that person out of a difficult situation. It was an amazing, responsible job.

Once I was called out to an incident where a man working in his garden had been stung all over his body by a swarm of wasps. When the ambulance arrived, he was close to collapse – his heart was racing and he couldn't breathe. There was no time to waste, so my partner and I rushed him into the back of the ambulance and started treating him as the sirens shrieked on the way to the hospital.

When we arrived in Accident and Emergency, he had revived and looked a million per cent better. The doctor was in no doubt that we had got to him in time and our actions had saved his life.

A year later a card arrived for me at the ambulance station, which was unusual. When I opened it, I saw a photograph of wasp man in a wedding suit beside his new wife. It read, "Thank you. Without you this would never have happened." Picking people up, calming them down, cheering them up and saving lives – that's what it was all about for me.

I was on duty in London on July 7, 2005 when the morning rush hour in the city was brought to a deadly standstill by suicide bombers. That day fifty-two people were killed and more than 770 people were injured as bombs ripped through London

Underground trains near Liverpool Street, Edgware Road and King's Cross stations and a bus in Tavistock Square. In the days that followed, there was an atmosphere of terror across the city as people living and working in London feared what might happen next. Medical staff worked hard to save the lives of those caught up in the attacks and an appeal was put out asking Londoners to avoid calling 999 unless it was really a life or death situation.

In the aftermath of the terror attacks, I realised, more than ever, I wanted to help our troops fighting the war in Iraq.

***

The one thing that had held me back from being a soldier was the asthma. Over the years I had visited several doctors who all said the same thing. But I got second and third opinions and eventually I was assessed by a specialist who uttered the magic words, "You haven't got asthma."

I was thrilled. But having cleared the one obstacle that stood in my way, I was confronted with another: my age. At thirty-seven I was too old to join the Regular Army, but the Army Reserve would take part-time soldiers up to the age of forty-three.

Having waited for so long, I was determined to sign up as soon as possible. My years of working as a paramedic gave me the expertise they needed out in the field, but I still had to complete all the basic mental and physical training. I used all my holidays and worked extra shifts on the ambulances to build up extra leave so that I could take time out to train.

First I had to be assessed to find out if I was strong and fit enough to join the Reserves. I was sent to the Army Training Centre in Pirbright along with dozens of other new recruits for a weekend selection.

To start with we had to carry two Jerry cans along a road to test our strength and grip. The cans were each filled with water weighing 20kg, and were designed to simulate the weight of fuel we would have to carry on operations. There was no room for dropping cans and spilling diesel in a war zone. We also had to lift a series of sandbags from the ground onto a platform above our heads. The bags went up in weight from 15kg through to 40kg - the maximum we would be expected to lift during operations. Finally we ran a mile and a half, and I managed it in thirteen minutes, a minute inside the time limit.

We were taken out marching with heavy backpacks on our backs, we crawled through mud, pulled ourselves across poles high above the ground and sprinted across fields. Each task was designed to test your upper and lower body strength and pick up any physical injuries or back problems that might stop you doing your job and put other soldiers at risk. As one of the oldest, and shortest of the new intake at 5ft 1in tall, I had a harder job than many of the younger, fitter recruits who were mostly men, but carrying patients in and out of ambulances for many years had prepared me well.

Although physical fitness is vital for a new recruit, mental agility is also important. We sat reading and maths tests, which showed we were capable of understanding and carrying out basic commands. The BARB (British Army Recruit Battery) test was a series of quick questions based around numbers, symbols, odd-one-out puzzles and reasoning to assess how well we could take in information and solve problems. The higher you scored in this test, the more jobs opportunities were available to you.

Flying through the assessments, the last step was the Oath of Allegiance. With the Bible in my left hand I swore to defend our Queen Elizabeth II and her successors against all enemies and obey all orders. And I was in! I was a private in an Army Reserve field hospital unit and was proud to be part of the Royal Army Medical Corps. I was one of the Corps' thousands of surgeons, pharmacists, doctors, dentists and medics who look after the troops at times of major traumas and disasters all over the world.

Now the job of becoming a real soldier began. I was packed off on a two-week crash course to the Army Training Centre in Sennybridge, Wales, followed by another two weeks at the ATC Grantham in Lincolnshire. I learnt how to stand to attention and march in hobnail boots. The officers took us on manoeuvres in the woods, where we spent the night making shelters and learning how to survive without our home comforts. I was taught how to maintain patrols, look after weapons and shoot a rifle. Everything pushed you to your physical limits.

Back at the camp there were lessons in the Army way of life, right down to making your bed to their strict neat standards, with hospital corners and pillowcases all facing the same way, and folding your clothes perfectly. Every day I would be put through my paces in the gym, with endless press-ups, sit-ups, squats, burpees and tricep dips. I could feel myself getting stronger and fitter by the day.

The final stage was to train in my specialist skill, which for me was the role of a combat medical technician and I would be taught all the procedures and medical skills I'd need to work in a war zone. As I was already working as a paramedic, I was fast-tracked through it all, taking only thirteen months to complete what would take a new recruit three years. When I was finally ready, I just had to wait for the next opportunity.

I returned to work on the ambulances, but was more desperate than ever to put my military training to use. Once a week I would join my local Reserve detachment for medical drills and practice and my weekends would be spent on training operations around the country. The more I was involved with the Army, the more I realised that a lot of my colleagues in the National Health Service also had links to the military. I couldn't help feeling envious when a paramedic shared stories about her husband who was serving in Afghanistan with the Reserves. At various hospitals I would meet doctors and nurses who had also been out helping the troops in the Middle East. There was something about the way they spoke, their posture, their manners, that gave them away. It was like a special lifesaving club.

All the time, the newspapers were filled with stories of soldiers being killed and injured in Afghanistan. The headlines screamed:

Two British soldiers killed by IED in Afghanistan.

Three British soldiers killed in Afghanistan when an armoured vehicle was devastated by a huge roadside bomb.

Lance Corporal killed by a gunshot wound during a firefight in Sangin.

Meanwhile I was getting called out to people who thought their headaches or bad backs were an emergency...

Our boys and girls are being blown up and I'm sat here on my bum waiting, I thought. I was becoming more and more frustrated. I wanted to be out in the desert using my medical expertise to care for the troops.

Soon I heard through the Reserve grapevine that 3 Medical Regiment was looking for Reserves to go on tour on Operation Herrick 17 in Afghanistan. The regiment provided all the main medical back-up on the ground. They ran the ambulance service and staffed a field hospital in Camp Bastion and more than a hundred other medical centres around the country. Knowing how desperate I was to get out there, my staff sergeant put my name forward and I was called for selection.

Naturally my friends and family were worried when I told them I had passed the tests and was ready to go to war.

"It's OK. I've worked in Brixton for so long, I'm sure I can handle Afghanistan," I reassured them.

"The Taliban don't care who they blow to pieces," my sister said.

Yet I wasn't worried. It was all I had ever wanted to do. That's why I signed up to the Reserves in the first place. I knew they needed medics on the ground and couldn't wait to get started.

"The troops will fight harder and fight well if they know their medical team is there for them. If I can stand there with those lads and they know I'm behind them with my weapon up to defend them and my medical kit on my back in case they get hurt – I'll be doing my job." That's what I told myself.

***

On the day of my thirty-ninth birthday in May 2012, I reported for duty at the regiment's barracks, which would be my home for the next two months until we were ready to deploy to Afghanistan.

I was living the dream. I was in the Army, working with the regular soldiers and living the Army life.

But despite my initial excitement, I was lonely.

The majority of the other soldiers were regulars and were half my age. Apart from our camouflage uniform, we had little in common. The thirty-somethings in the garrison were officers and it wasn't the done thing for a lower rank to socialise with the superiors. I started to miss my family back home.

On top of that I was also a novice when it came to soldiering. The majority of the other recruits at my level had been in the Army for a couple of years, so they could do all the drills perfectly and knew all the commands. Everything that they took for granted, I struggled with. I would turn up at the wrong place with the wrong equipment. Even little things like packing our bergans (rucksacks) I did badly. I looked over at the other soldiers and all their kit and sleeping bags were packed neatly into their small rucksacks. Mine looked like an explosion in a camouflage factory.

On one exercise we were training with bayonets, running up a hill and back down when the captain yelled a comment about my age. I tried not to take it personally but I felt as if the other soldiers were looking at me and thinking, What the hell have we got here? Another time he shouted at me because I was wearing the wrong belt. Sometimes he would bark his orders and I would look at him with a blank expression as I had no idea what he meant. As you can imagine it didn't go down well.

It all fed my insecurity and made me think, What am I doing here? I can't do this. But I kept on telling myself, "You've fought hard to get here. Put your chin up and get on with it. You can do this." It made me more determined to keep up with all the young recruits, even if I was blowing like a whale as I did.

There was so much to learn, in such a short time. But I got fitter and stronger and by the deployment date, I was ready. After all the final checks I was handed my metal dog tags inscribed with my name, service number, date of birth and blood group. If I was blown to bits, these two pieces of metal would be the way the Army would identify my body and would break the bad news to my next of kin. This was real.

***

My first taste of the desert heat came as I stepped off the military plane at Camp Bastion. The hot, arid air hit me like a hairdryer in the face. We'd been travelling all day in the hold of a cargo plane and I was just looking forward to my bed.

Bastion was like a town in the desert. At the height of the war it had been home to almost 30,000 British and American soldiers and had its own hospital, shops and police force. It even had a Pizza Hut, housed in a shipping container. All troops arriving in Afghanistan spent their first week in Camp Bastion getting used to working in the fifty degree temperatures.

I was shown to a tent near the airfield, where rows of bunks were laid out. It didn't look comfortable, but it was somewhere to put my head down for the night. I laid out my sleeping bag and bedded down.

The next morning as we were getting ready to move on to the medical staff section near the hospital, a young soldier came up to my bed and introduced herself.

"Hi, I'm Tash. We're going to be posted together down at Patrol Base in Durai," she said.

"Awesome," I replied.

Tash had an open, smiley face and a warm

Scottish accent. As an outsider, it was wonderful to make friends before being sent out to a hostile environment.

Chapter Five

Arrival in Afghanistan

'Life, limbs and eyesight' – those were the rules for all the medics at the medical centre in Durai. We were the closest centre to the front line that had a doctor on duty, so we saw all kinds of injuries and illnesses. But our main priorities were treating those with eye injuries that could make them blind or in danger of losing the use of their arms or legs.

Mornings would be like a regular doctor's surgery with what we called 'sick parade'. Soldiers would come in to see the doctor and medical sergeant with their ailments. With temperatures reaching an unbearable fifty degrees in the summer months, it was quite common to see men suffering from dizziness and headaches – the warning signs of dehydration. Others would be suffering from diarrhoea or sickness or may have sprained ankles or twisted shoulders in accidents around the camp.

There was an area with beds, where we

could nurse soldiers back to health so they could return to duty. More serious cases would be flown by helicopter to the field hospital at Camp Bastion.

When I first started the Scots Guards were based on camp, and I was so relieved that Tash was working with me. They spoke in such thick accents, I couldn't understand what they were saying. I would often look over at Tash and mouth, "Translation please?"

Our main job was keeping our troops healthy and out of pain, but local people would often bring their sick and injured children to us in desperation. A young local girl was attacked by a dog and her father, an Afghan farmer, came to us in panic. We calmed him down, treated the wounds and referred him back to his own doctor. We were aware that we had to make them more reliant on their own services as we would not always be there for them.

On another occasion a thirteen-year-old homeless beggar was rushed into our base by the local police after he was hit by a car on the streets around Lashkar Gah. His heart had stopped and although we tried to bring him back by pumping his chest and attempting to restart his heart with electrical pulses from a defibrillator, it was useless. He had gone.

As I zipped his young body into a bag, I noticed the soles of his bare feet were so hardened from walking on the desert ground, which was caked like red-hot cement, that they had formed a thick outer layer. His feet looked like he was wearing shoes – but it was his skin. Working on the ambulances, I had seen most things – but never anything like that. The state of that poor boy's feet will stay in my head for ever. He had nothing. Not even anyone to care that he had passed away.

It was the first time our medical team had experienced the death of someone so young and it affected them badly. No-one takes into account what young soldiers have to witness. I knew soldiers who watched their friends and colleagues die from horrific bomb and gunshot injuries. Some tried to take their own lives as a result of the Post Traumatic Stress Disorder (PTSD) they suffered after being exposed to these terrible things. I was lucky. I had all those years of working with London Ambulance and had dealt with most things. Sadly there was very little I hadn't seen before.

If only we had known then that this was just the start. There was worse to come.

When Tash and I returned to camp one afternoon after being out on our regular patrols with the Scots Guards, the head of our centre called us to one side.

"You had better take a seat. We have some bad news," he said.

Tash and I froze.

"There have been two fatalities." The news hit us like a kick to the guts.

"A medic was killed this afternoon while out on patrol with a Royal Marine," he continued. I looked at Tash as the colour drained from under her helmet.

It was one of our own. A Combat Medical Technician like us. We were told they had been on their way to teach first aid to the Afghan Local Police when they were shot at and killed. Just a few weeks earlier we had all been together training before leaving for Afghanistan.

"Medics are not meant to die," Tash sobbed. As her 'Tour Mum' I tried to comfort her by telling her that they had died doing a job they loved, defending their country. I also felt a strange sense of guilt. It could have been any one of us.

Little did I know the impact such bad news headlines was having back home. One of my close friends was on the train to work, when she saw the headline MEDIC KILLED IN AFGHANISTAN on the newspaper a man opposite her was reading. Throughout the journey she struggled to get a closer look at it across the packed carriage. Eventually, in utter panic, she grabbed the newspaper. When she saw the photo she burst into tears and screamed, "It's not her! It's not her!" while all the commuters turned and stared.

I only found out about this incident when I returned home and it made me realise just how worried my friends were. Whenever a fatality happened during operations a news blackout was put on all troops until the next of kin were officially informed. My close family knew I was safe, but I hadn't thought about my wider circle of friends. It was a weird sensation, but would not change my actions to serve my country.

It's hard to lose one of your own. But we couldn't let it get to us. We had a job to do. The next morning we were back out on patrol.

***

One of the worst things about being a woman in the Army was the toilet situation on patrol. It was all right for the boys, they could use empty bottles. How often I wished my bladder was the size of a hot air balloon!

On one occasion I was the only woman in the back of an armoured Warrior AFV, out with American troops searching an area around Helmand Province for Taliban hideouts and explosives. I had been holding it in for eight hours and got to the point where it was almost painful to move.

"I really need a pee," I begged the Sgt Major.

"I can't let you out now," he barked. It was too dangerous. The ground was peppered with roadside bombs and there could have been snipers hiding, waiting to pick off the enemy at an unguarded moment. I just had to sit and suffer for a while longer. With every bump and judder, I winced more.

When I finally had the command "Go now" from the Sgt Major, the Warrior was at a halt. I didn't need to be told a second time. I threw my weight at the heavy door, hurled myself onto the ground and squatted down beside the Warrior, camouflage trousers in a wrinkled heap around my boots.

Suddenly I felt the ground shake as the engine started and the vehicle began to move.

"Get in the vehicle now," the Sgt Major ordered as I pulled up my pants and chased after my unit, not caring that the American Marines following behind got a full rear view of my pasty arse. I threw myself through the opening and slammed the door shut behind me with a bang.

Boom! There was another loud noise – our vehicle had run over an IED. A second later and I could have run over it and been blown to pieces with my pants down. I was shaken, but I couldn't stop giggling as I imagined the expressions on the faces of the American troops. "Now that's what you call bringing up the rear," I laughed to myself.

Back at base I was sitting outside the medical centre, telling Tash my story, when Vidar and his handler Tom walked by.

"Hello, Vidar," I said, jumping up to waggle his ears and rub his back. "I hope you haven't shamed yourself today like I have," I said.

Suddenly he shot off.

"What's up with him? Was it something I said?" I asked Tom.

"There must be a helicopter coming in."

Sure enough, within seconds the deafening "whacker, whacker" noise filled the air and the sandy rotor blades of a Merlin appeared, coming in to land on the airpad behind the medical centre. Tom didn't seem at all bothered that his dog had legged it.

"He'll be hiding under my bed. Hates the noise of helicopters," Tom explained.

Poor Vidar, I thought. If he wanted to get away from helicopters he was in the wrong job.

***

In January I got my 'R&R' rest and recuperation break – two weeks to go back home to Barry and see my friends and family. But after months of being at camp, being able to play with the working dogs, the house felt empty without a furry companion. So I decided I would find out how I could adopt Vidar.

One of the dog handlers in Afghanistan had given me a copy of a letter to use for a 'Live Cast' request, which is the term the military give to rehoming their trained dogs. Often the handlers would get so close to their dogs that they would take them home once they retired, but for Vidar and Tom that wasn't an option.

So I sat down and wrote...

To Whom It May Concern,

I, Lance Corporal Angie McDonnell, would like to place my application to live cast Military Working Dog VIDAR when his service career is over.

I am currently deployed in Afghanistan on Op HERRICK 17 in Durai as a Combat Medical Technician but live in Wales.

I have spent a lot of time with Vidar down in Durai and have grown very fond of him. I have past experience of owning German shepherds, not to mention a multitude of cats, gerbils and any other four-legged strays that wandered too close to my house. I take a keen interest in anything to do with the handling and training and also the healthcare of dogs. If successful in my application, Vidar would have the run of the house and a garden to enjoy. I am also within a short distance of Brecon and the Welsh countryside.

I am a keen runner and walker; I would love to be able to take Vidar with me to give him that quiet and enjoyable space and fresh air he so thoroughly deserves in his retirement.

I would have no problem in arranging a viewing of my home to make sure I am a suitable candidate. I believe he would be very happy with me and have a comfortable lifestyle upon his retirement.

I understand that all medical and veterinary bills would become my responsibility and adequate pet insurance will have to be put in place.

Yours truly,
Lance Corporal Angie McDonnell
Senior paramedic

I posted my letter off to the Defence Animal Centre in Melton Mowbray, where all the working dogs end up before being rehomed. I didn't even know what Vidar's future in the Army was going to be. All I hoped was that if the rumours were true and he was no longer able to do his job, he would have a happy retirement home with me.

Chapter Six
"Bye Bye, Bastion"

By the middle of April my time in Afghanistan was coming to an end and I was looking forward to flying back home to Wales. It had been weeks since I had seen Vidar. His handler had moved on to another operation and there was a new dog in his kennel.

"I really miss my boy, you know," I said to Tash one afternoon as we were packing up our kit and preparing for our flights back to Camp Bastion before returning to the UK. "Do you think I'll ever see him again?"

"Course you will. You've told them that you can give him a home, you'll just have to be patient and keep your fingers crossed."

There was a rumour that Vidar had been moved to the Military Working Dogs kennels at Camp Bastion, which made me even more eager to leave camp. When I finally arrived at Bastion, I began my search.

The Military Working Dogs Regiment was based at Bastion. There the dogs were cared for as well, if not better, than the soldiers. They had luxury kennels with fluffy white beds and air-conditioning for the days when temperatures shot up to a sweltering fifty degrees, and central heating for the nights when the temperature dropped to minus ten. At the height of the war, there were 150 teams of dogs and handlers at the compound. They had fenced off areas of desert where they trained the dogs to sniff out IEDs, which were also used as exercise yards. There was a hydrotherapy plunge pool to help the animals cool down and a surgery with vets and nurses to take care of any injuries and for routine medical checks, just like their human colleagues.

The MWD compound stood out from other military areas in Bastion partly because of the howling but also it had a bright red paw on the sign. I got off the bus outside and was met by one of the trainers.

"I'm trying to find 'Boggles'," I said, using the nickname Vidar's handlers had given him because of the way his eyes popped out on stalks like a cartoon character every time he heard a loud noise.

"He's down at the other kennels," the trainer said and pointed out the location on a map. So I set off across camp.

A chorus of growls let me know that I was getting close. Inside the kennels German shepherds and Mallies paced their runs, setting off a chain reaction of ferocious barking which rippled along the line of white-painted kennels.

At the far end a dog was going mental. He was spinning in circles, jumping at the bars, howling.

I knew it was Vidar.

"Can I go in and see him?" I asked the handler on duty. He looked at me as if I had a death wish.

"Are you absolutely sure that's the right dog?" He hesitated as Vidar continued to throw himself at the bars.

"That's Vidar all right." I was certain. He was smaller than other Mallies and even through his crazy behaviour, I could see the softie I remembered from Durai.

Warily the handler approached his cage.

"Hey, Vidar," I called. He stopped spinning and cocked his head to one side.

Cautiously the handler hooked a lead onto Vidar's collar. He began to go wild again, jumping up at the lead and tying himself and the handler in knots. He lunged forward on his lead and at that moment I panicked. What if I had the wrong dog and this one was trained to attack strangers? I was quite fond of my arms.

I wasn't expecting him to remember me, but when he saw me he dragged the handler towards me. It was like he was in slow-motion. His front paws were off the ground and he was straining on his leash.

I dropped to my knees and he pounced on me, thumping his big brown paws on my shoulders. I ruffled his fur and he licked my ears. It was as if we had never been separated.

"So what's going to happen to him?" I asked the handler.

"He's going to be retired from duty. He's definitely gun shy."

"But where will he go?"

"All depends," the handler said. "If he can be retrained, they'll try and find him a new home." He shrugged.

"I'm going to give him a home." I worried that not everyone would see the soppy sausage underneath the frightened and erratic exterior and he might not get the home he deserved.

"I'll take care of you, my boy," I promised, giving him a final kiss on the top of his head. I watched him lollop back down the walkway to his kennel, a much calmer dog than the one I had seen only minutes before. I was more determined than ever that this dog, who had protected me and so many of my friends, should have a chance of a happy future.

Chapter Seven
Saving Vidar

Some people say that a house is not a home unless it has a dog. I missed having the Army dogs around me. I had given up my job in the ambulance service to move to south Wales, so I had plenty of time on my hands. But walking and running through the fields and roads around my home felt empty without a dog by my side. I wished I was back in Afghanistan, sitting with the sniffer spaniels and asking them, "What have you found today?"

Most of all, I missed Vidar.

I tried to find out what was happening to him. I asked my friends in the Army and eventually I found out the name of the officer in charge of the rehoming unit at the Defence Animal Centre in Melton Mowbray. I sat down and wrote another letter, this time hoping it would get to the right person.

Dear Sir,

I write to you today in reference to MWD Vidar.

I met Vidar back in Durai; I am a Combat Medical Technician in the Reserve Army. Whilst on tour Vidar displayed behaviour that indicated he was 'gun and bang shy' and subsequently was returned to the UK and to you in Melton Mowbray. I have already written a letter for Vidar's file requesting to rehome him and I understand that the paperwork would now be ready for signing off.

I am very keen to give Vidar a loving and active home. I have been in constant touch with your staff enquiring on his progress and wellbeing. I have also taken a great deal of time to study and learn about training and living with a working dog. I have thought very carefully about my home and how to make it safer for him as well as how to integrate him safely within my family. I am very keen (should you agree I can rehome him) to maintain a full and enjoyable quality of life for him within a safe, happy and loving environment which I feel he thoroughly deserves after the service he has given.

Although I fully understand the workings of the British Army, I would be very keen to have Vidar in my home as soon as possible in order to allow him to adapt. Also I'm sure the resources at Melton could be much better used on the dogs you can work and train as it must cost a considerable sum to be keeping Vidar and not be able to use him to any benefit yourselves.

I would be very grateful for any help you could give me in this matter. He is a wonderful little dog and I really would love to have him home before Christmas.

I look forward to hearing from you.

Kind regards,

Angie McDonnell

A week passed. No reply. I followed up with email after email after email: still no response. Finally I found a phone number for the rehoming centre and rang. To my embarrassment it was the direct line to the centre's senior commanding officer, not the general office, as I had thought.

"Oh, sir," I stuttered. "I'm so sorry. I seem to

have come through to you by mistake."

"So how can I help you?"

I explained the situation. How I had fallen for Vidar and was desperate to make sure he had a good home to live out his final years.

"Give me ten minutes and someone will call you back," the officer said.

True to his word, a Major from the training centre called and asked, "What can we do to get this sorted?"

"I'd like my dog, please!" I said rather cheekily.

He confirmed that Vidar had recently arrived in the kennels at Melton Mowbray. After his tour of duty ended in Afghanistan he had been sent back to the Military Working Dogs unit in Germany to readjust after working in the scorching desert heat. It was there that they confirmed he was 'gun shy', took him out of active service and returned him to the UK.

"His temperament is excellent, so we are able to use him to train the new dog handler recruits," the Major explained.

That came as a blow. I had assumed there would be no use for him in the Army. But at least he still had a job to do, so I was happy for him.

"Please will you keep my letter on file," I

pleaded with the officer. "If and when the time comes for him to retire, will you call me?"

"Yes, that's not a problem."

I had done all I could. There was no point chasing it any longer. I hung up, not entirely convinced that I would ever hear from them again. It could be years before he would retire. In the meantime I consoled myself by surfing the internet to learn more about working dogs. I joined an online networking site for the owners of working dogs across Europe, just like Facebook but for working dogs, and uncovered more about their training. And I read up more about the breed that I had come to admire. Most experts described them as high-energy with a sharp mind. I already knew that – I had seen him at work. I understood they needed a firm leader who could give them the exercise and training they required to keep their bodies and minds active and stop them becoming dominant towards other dogs. There was no point in me offering to take responsibility for a dog like Vidar if I wasn't going to be fully committed to his ongoing training. I didn't want him to end up in another kennel or having to be put to sleep because he had become aggressive or destructive. I wanted him to have the best chance.

Two months later, I got a phone call.

"You put in a letter to adopt Vidar?"

"I did," I confirmed.

"He seems to have a problem with his eyesight, he's been walking into fences. Would you still be interested in taking him?"

"Of course I still want him," I said with certainty. I was aware that he might be having trouble seeing things from some of the conversations I had with handlers in Afghanistan. Progressive Retinal Atrophy (PRA) was a common problem with some dog breeds and around one in every ten Mallies got it. It was a condition that was passed down through the parents and affected the lining at the back of the eye. At four years old Vidar was quite young to be suffering from it. It wasn't painful. But there was no cure and eventually he would go blind.

"We're getting one of our specialist vets to check him out and we'll be in contact when we have more information."

That's good news for me, isn't it? I thought, knowing that if he couldn't see he wouldn't be much good for working with the trainee handlers.

Finally, a few weeks later, I got the news I had been waiting six months to hear.

"We are retiring Vidar. He's no longer fit for service, so he's all yours."

Chapter Eight
Ready for Retirement

What does a dog of determination and courage need? A bed to call his own, bowls for his food and water and toys to keep his mind stimulated. With my shopping list, I set off for the local pet store to prepare for the new arrival.

There was so much to choose from. Wooden puzzles which worked the dog's brain as they sniffed out treats; plastic toys in the shape of Bourbon chocolate biscuits or false teeth; fluffy pheasants that honked when you squeezed their beaks. There were even balls with motors which moved on their own to really confuse your pet. But for a tough boy like Vidar I opted for some tough toys: a sturdy red rubber Kong, which I could fill with food and treats, a leather football to play with in the fields and a heavy-duty ball on a rope to play tug-o-war.

I also stocked up on the premium brand of dried food which he had been fed on throughout his Army life. The trainers at the rehoming centre had advised me to stick to the same diet to avoid problems with runny tummies.

When it came to the beds there was just as much choice as the toys. There were soft, squishy beds lined with thick fur, jumbo floor cushions covered in corduroy, big brown paw-shaped pads. One bed was shaped like a leather sofa and had a price tag higher than the cost of my own furniture! I considered buying the biggest metal cage they had, but decided against it. He had spent his life in kennels, he deserved some freedom. I saw a Union Jack cushion, which could have been perfect for a dog that had served his country, but instead I chose what I thought would suit him best – a bright pink plastic bed. And to make sure he was comfortable I bought a sheepskin-covered memory foam mattress to lay inside it.

***

I set off on the 180-mile trip to the English market town of Melton Mowbray. All I could think of was Vidar. It had been almost six months since we said goodbye in Camp Bastion and I wondered if he would recognise me.

The Defence Animal Centre is massive, sprawling over 346 acres of green fields and paddocks. Home to the Royal Army Veterinary Corps, it is a centre of excellence for training all animals in the Ministry of Defence and the soldiers who work with them. It is the main base for the Vet Training Squadron, who look after the health of the military animals, and the Equine Training Squadron which trains all the horses and riders of the Household Cavalry and King's Troop Royal Horse Artillery, which you see flanking the Queen and VIPs on official ceremonies. It is also where the Canine Training Squadron teaches new dog handlers how to work with and look after their Military Working Dogs.

To prepare for Vidar's arrival, I had been in contact with his trainer at the rehoming centre, who had given me tips on how to handle an ex-military dog. It was her job to de-train the dogs to prepare them for retirement. These animals had only ever known life in Army kennels, so she had to assess them to make sure they had the right temperament and were physically capable of living in a family home.

At the centre they vetted potential new owners to be certain they were able to take on the training that a former working dog would need, and had the patience and understanding to help the animal to adjust to its new setting.

They also checked how the dogs reacted with other members of the family and pets and looked at how secure the new owners' gardens were.

Sadly not all dogs are able to be rehomed. The cute Springer spaniels and Labradors are usually top of the list for rehoming. But some patrol dogs have a temperament that is too dangerous to retrain and others have serious health issues. It is these animals that end up being put to sleep.

Vidar had been assessed for any aggression that might have caused problems when I got him home. The rehoming trainers brushed his fur, pulled up his jowls and looked at his teeth, ran their hands all over his body, lifted his paws and felt his joints and bottom. They had to make sure he would be tolerant when I took him to the vet or dog groomers. They tested his patience by pulling his ears and grabbing him, just as a young child might do in the outside world.

At the centre they also had an area where the dogs could be introduced to the noises and smells of a house. It was set up like a regular home and had a living room with a sofa and TV and a kitchen with a table and chairs and a washing machine. Here Vidar had spent his first night watching *EastEnders* and sleeping indoors.

The trainers had taken him to a pond within the grounds and let him loose to find out if he was afraid of water, which he wasn't. Then they took him out walking on a lead with other dogs and their handlers to see how he would react as he was so used to working on his own as an IED sniffer dog.

As I approached the kennels, my stomach twisted. I was so excited. From the first time I'd seen him in Afghanistan, I knew we were meant to be together. It felt so right. I sensed he had the soul of a saint in the body of a military dog. And I had a lovely home waiting for 'my boy'.

But I was also a bit nervous. What if I'd got it wrong and he turned out to be a lunatic? "Don't be an idiot," I told myself. "The trainers know what they are doing. If he was bad they wouldn't let him go."

The trainer met me in the car park and walked me down to the kennel, where Vidar was going nuts, bouncing against the bars of the kennel as usual.

"Vidar," I called. And he stopped, cocked his head to one side and looked as if he was saying, "I know that voice." He had that same boggle-eyed expression I remembered, the one that said, "Please love me." At that moment I knew I was doing the right thing.

"I think he remembers you," the trainer said, handing me his lead and opening the door that was separating us.

When he saw the lead, Vidar jumped up and tried to grab it.

"Don't let him do that. He will tug you down the road," she warned. I stood still until he stopped bouncing around like a mad thing. When he was calm, I said "Come on" and tried to walk towards the training field. But he just stood there, completely ignoring me. This is a good start, I thought.

"You'll need to be more forceful," the trainer explained.

Walking down to the field, he pulled and jumped. Every time he misbehaved, I stopped and waited until he was calm before continuing our walk.

"Good," the trainer said, giving me tips to help me teach Vidar. I was used to the discipline and determination of military drills, so I was looking forward to learning new things together.

"He's not a dog's dog," the trainer warned me. "Make sure other dogs don't get too close to him and train him on his own, away from other animals."

For an hour Vidar ran around the field

burning off his boundless energy. "He'll take as much exercise as you can give him. You can never give a Mallie too much," I was told.

"Have you been told about the PRA?" the trainer asked, handing me a letter from the veterinary eye specialist which explained how his eye condition would get worse with age. "He can't see anything out of the top half of his eyes." To demonstrate she hurled his bright blue ball into the air. He bounded off in the opposite direction, then came to a halt with a baffled expression that said, "What have you done with it?" When she rolled the ball along the ground, he was straight on it, no problem.

"You'll need to be aware of his sight problems when you take him for walks in places where there are other dogs and people, so he doesn't get frightened," she explained. There was so much to take in.

"So do you still want him?"

I screwed up my face. "Nah, I'm not sure. Let him go to Death Row." I paused, waiting for the reaction. "Course I friggin' want him."

****

In the rehoming centre I filled out the necessary forms, paid a £5 Live Cast request fee to cover the cost of transferring his ownership to me, and he was mine.

As we made our way back to the car, I passed

a couple of dog handlers. "Are you Vidar's new mum?" they asked. Obviously news travelled fast in military dog land.

"Enjoy your new life in Wales, old boy," they said, patting his muscular rump.

I opened the back door of my car for him to hop in. The trainer was horrified.

"Are you sure you want to do this?" she asked, eyeing up my shiny new VW Golf, with its immaculate seat covers and that fresh-out-of-the-garage smell. The other dog handlers laughed knowingly.

Shit! I thought. What if he doesn't like travelling in cars? I had visions of a Turner and Hooch moment. You know, the scene in the film where that big, slobbery mastiff starts ripping apart the car seats and his new owner Tom Hanks shouts, "Don't eat the car!"

"Good luck," the trainer smirked. "If you get any problems, just call."

I can honestly say that that journey back to Wales felt longer than the flight to Afghanistan. Every tiny noise I thought was him chewing my car. I kept checking in my rear view mirror but mostly he just yawned and stretched. It was a tough life, being an Army dog in retirement.

Chapter Nine
Not a Dog's Dog

Training began before we even walked into the house. I made him sit outside the front door while I went in. "Come on in," I invited him. It was important that I showed him who was top dog and by making him wait, not only was I teaching him good manners, but I was giving the signal that I was going to be leader of this pack.

Gingerly he stepped into the hallway. His big black nose, more used to sniffing out guns and explosives, was now picking up all sorts of new smells. The mud on my walking boots in the corner, the scent of grass on my coat. He started panting, a sign that he was feeling nervous and unsettled. I could see the tip of his long, pink tongue flickering. It was all new to him.

"It's OK, boy. This is your new home."

He looked at me, whale-eyed, a white moon shape in the corner of his eyes. It was another sign he was getting stressed. I backed off to give him time to get his bearings. His paws were used to walking on the hot, hard orange dust of the desert floor, so I wasn't sure how they would react to the woolliness of a carpet. But he seemed to take it all in his stride.

When I could see he was more relaxed, I showed him to his new bed, which was next to the sofa in the front room.

I know they say dogs are colour-blind, which isn't exactly true, but I swear he took one look at the dog basket and said, "What the f***! Do I look like a pink pussy?" Then just to show how much I had offended his masculinity, he lay down on the floor in front of it with his head turned as far away from it as he could.

In the garden, his nose shot into the air. My neighbour had a bull terrier and Vidar's highly trained nose could sense there was another dog around. He made a beeline for the fence, dragging his leathery nose along the boundary, taking in all the new scents.

When a cat hopped over the back wall and into the garden, my heart stopped. I expected him to pounce on it as he had never seen one before, but he just sat and watched while it crapped all over my marigolds.

By evening he seemed more comfortable in his new surroundings. He had wolfed down his dried food and, putting his embarrassment aside, settled into his new bed.

That night I hardly slept. I was listening out for any tell-tale noises that he might be eating my kitchen. I was ready to run downstairs at any minute and find Vidar sitting in a pile of wrappers and wooden splinters and a hole where my food cupboard had been. But there was nothing, not even a whimper.

In the morning, he was in exactly the same position as I had left him, lying at an angle in his basket, legs outstretched touching one end, head squashed up against the other end.

"Good morning," I said, tickling the one bat ear that was sticking out. "Sleep well?"

He stretched his legs out even further and shook his head as if to say, "Do you mind, I'm comfortable."

The following night, I slept easier knowing that he was settling into his bed. But in the middle of the night I felt a movement and a warm, furry lump against my left side. He had slunk up onto my bed and that's where he stayed. It hadn't taken him long to make himself at home.

For a dog that had only known the concrete floors of kennels, Vidar was getting remarkably settled in his new home. But every day there was something new to challenge him and bring out the boggle-eyed stare.

The first time he heard a bang from the washing machine, he legged it and I had to coax him out from behind the sofa with his ball. When the doorbell rang, he sat completely still and looked confused. He didn't have the instinct to run towards it barking like other dogs. When friends visited, he just lay on the floor and looked at them. There was a fine line between being protective and being a complete wuss. He had never really had an area to protect, so it took him time to adjust to having his bed and his space. Yet I didn't want to encourage him to become too protective. On the rare occasions he would get possessive over one of his toys, I would firmly tell him "No" and stop him. I was aware that I had to keep him disciplined but also allow him to relax in his retirement and be like a normal pet dog. I was the boss and he had to follow the rules.

Once he was comfortable on his own turf, it was time to explore new places. I was lucky that I lived close to the coast, so we spent an afternoon chasing his football along the shoreline. But as soon as he heard the waves crashing, his eyes started to boggle and he ran away from the noise. He probably couldn't see the waves but the noise frightened him.

It wasn't long before I understood what the trainers meant when they told me Vidar was "not a dog's dog". I started taking him out with a friend and her Springer spaniel and as long as they kept their distance walking alongside each other on a lead, Vidar was calm and happy. But in public places like the park and the beach, I was always conscious of other dogs. The problem was the other owners who didn't understand the concept of personal doggy space. Whenever we came across other dogs on a walk, I would call, "Foot – heel, Vidar." It sounded confusing to any other dog walkers, but he always got the message and ran back to my side so I could put his lead back on. His obedience was spot-on.

Unfortunately other owners weren't as well trained.

"It's all right, he loves other dogs," they would shout as their energetic pooch bounded towards Vidar.

"But... but..." Too late. The dog was nose to nose with Vidar and he showed them his ferocious fangs. Usually this was enough to send the friendly dogs packing. But there were occasions when the other dog took offence and it would end up in a scrap.

One day I was bending down to pick up Vidar's mess, when a German shepherd ran over and started sniffing his butt. Vidar spun around so quickly that he lost his footing and slipped on the grass. The German shepherd ran off, much to my relief, as I had very little chance of protecting myself in a dog fight carrying a bag full of poo.

The problem was Vidar didn't understand dog behaviour. As a pup he had never been socialised properly with other dogs and had never learnt that butt-sniffing is the normal way of getting to know another dog, like humans shaking hands or high-fiving. Dogs' noses are up to 100,000 times more sensitive than humans' and a whiff of the rear end will tell them a lot about the other animal.

In Vidar's partially sighted world he saw a dog in his space as a threat and his natural reaction was to tell them to back off.

In these dog fights, Vidar wasn't always to blame. We were out playing football in a field one morning when a collie dog hurled itself towards us and clamped onto Vidar's back leg. Naturally Vidar resisted and before I could call him to heel, hackles were up, fur was flying and teeth were clashing. I looked around but couldn't see anyone with the other dog.

"Vidar, stop!" I shouted and, always obedient, he did. But it was no use. The collie carried on and Vidar was forced to fight back.

Both dogs were getting stuck in and I ended up being caught in the middle as I foolishly tried to separate them.

Finally the owner appeared and called the collie away. By that time my hands were covered in bite marks. And Vidar just looked up at me and wagged his tail as if to say, "Come on, Mum, let's play."

Chapter Ten
The Perfect Pet

Vidar is a dog of constant surprises. It makes me laugh when I think how worried I was on the day I collected him from the kennels. I should have trusted my instincts. He is one of the cleanest dogs I have ever known. He has never had an accident in the house and he has never chewed anything – not even his squeaky toys. He doesn't have it in him to be destructive.

All was going well and he seemed to be settling well into his new life. His soppiness was earning him new friends everywhere we went. I started taking him with me to my Reserve Army Centre, where he would be fussed over by all the other soldiers.

But a flashback from his past came back to haunt him. Out on a walk one afternoon, Vidar suddenly froze in his tracks. His ears shot up in the air and his eyes started to boggle. He started panting and was about to run away from me.

Whacker, whacker, whacker. I looked up and spotted a military helicopter hovering above our heads.

Our house was close to the Royal Air Force training base at St Athan and it was not unusual for aircraft to pass over, but Vidar didn't know that.

"It's all right, mate. You're not getting on that helicopter," I tried to reassure him. But he didn't understand. In his mind he was going to be whisked back into the turmoil of war with all its gunfire and explosions.

At other times when we were out together, I'd hear the guns of the military firing range in the distance and expect him to react. But those bangs didn't seem to bother him. As long as they were far enough away, he didn't mind. It was just those damned low-flying helicopters that stressed him out.

I tried to change our routine to avoid the times when I thought the helicopters would be around. But it wasn't easy to gauge. If I heard a helicopter coming I would try to head for home, but we didn't always make it in time. As they clattered past us, Vidar would freeze.

Bonfire Night was approaching too. As soon as he heard the ear-piercing whizzes and thunderous bangs of rockets exploding in the skies around our house, days before November fifth, it reminded him of the grenades and gunshots in Afghanistan. It was heart-breaking to see him so stressed and panting so hard I thought he was going to pass out. I felt so sorry for him and so useless. I tried climbing into his bed with him and cuddling him, but it didn't stop him being scared.

When Bonfire Night came, to escape the endless explosions he ran into the garden and in a panic tried to scratch his way out under the fence and onto a busy road. It was the final straw. I couldn't risk him putting his life in danger. Something had to change.

I called his trainer at the Army rehoming centre for some advice. I explained what had happened and how he was reacting.

"I have to do something. I don't want him to always be scared of noises and associate it with war and fighting," I told her.

"It's only natural that you want to reassure him and calm him down. But that's not actually helping him," she explained. "You're telling him that it's OK to be scared. What you need to do is distract him with something he enjoys. You need to change his thought process so instead of being scared of loud noises he associates them with something good. What does he like?"

Unlike most dogs, Vidar had never really been motivated by food. But he loved to play.

"So you distract him with his toys," the trainer suggested. "But you have to be one step ahead. You need to get the ball out and get him engaged before he hears the noises and starts his stress cycle."

The next time we were out, I made sure I carried his bright orange rubber ball with me. When I heard the drone of a helicopter in the distance, I ignored it and threw his ball for him. At first he was torn between being scared and chasing the toy. But over time he began to focus more of his attention onto his toy and less on the noise above his head. It was great progress. Now if he hears a helicopter, he looks at me and waits for me to throw his toy. It's taken time but he can now associate the noise with fun and games, not guns and bombs.

Fireworks are still a work-in-progress. If we are outdoors and he hears a firework bang, he will run back to the house, so I have learnt to keep him indoors. Once he's safe in the house, he can cope with the noise. He'll jump at first, but then he'll look at me and if I don't react, he will look back towards the direction of the noise and settle down. He's never going to want to go to a fireworks display but I can live with that.

He can be such a nervous ninny - if someone touches him from behind he jumps out of his skin. So I always tell people to walk in front of him, where he can see them, and then say hello. I don't want him to be frightened. I feel it's my duty to protect him.

His failing eyesight doesn't help when other dogs are around. I have a scar on my right hand where I had to step in to stop him turning on a little Cavalier King Charles spaniel that ran up to him from behind. The owner wasn't impressed by Vidar's reaction to her docile little dog, who only wanted to say hello. But again it comes down to the ignorance of other owners. Just because their dog is placid and friendly doesn't mean all dogs are, and they should keep them under control in open spaces - or be ready to face the consequences.

These days if I see a dog running towards us, I will get Vidar's ball out and get him to focus on that. Sometimes it will distract him long enough for me to shoo the other dog away before he warns them off.

But even that has its problems. One evening Vidar was off his lead. I was kicking his white football across the field and he was fetching it. We'd been out for a while and the light was fading. I was thinking it was time to go home, but Vidar kept coming back, tossing his ball around in the air. He was having great fun. He'd drop his ball at my feet, wag his tail, and look up at me with his great pink tongue flopping out as if to say, "Please, Mum. Just one more throw."

So we carried on playing. I kicked his ball across the field and he chased it into the distance. All of a sudden I noticed a car pull up and a woman got out and put something down on the ground. From where I was standing, it looked like a white handbag. A split second later the handbag moved. It was a fluffy white Pomeranian, no bigger than Vidar's ball, and it was making a beeline for him.

Before I had a chance to call him to heel, Vidar had the 'furry ball' in his mouth. He was running around the field, ragging it on the ground, thinking it was a toy. I couldn't chase him as he would just think it was a game and would run further away, but I had to get him to drop it. He was having great fun. The owner not so much; she was horrified. "Leave!" I shouted and Vidar dropped it. The poor animal was a quivering mess of mud, fur and Mallie saliva. I picked it up and handed it back to its owner.

That's when I realised she was one of the

officers at my Reserve unit.

"I'm so sorry, Ma'am. Is your dog OK?" I asked. "He thought your dog was his football." I felt I needed to speak up in Vidar's defence.

Gently she checked her pet all over and miraculously there was not a mark on him, except for the dirt and dribble. Thank God.

Vidar is ball mad and, until he loses his sight completely, always will be. Footballs, tennis balls, rubber balls, he's not fussy. It's a never-ending game to him. He'll chase them through long grass, over sand, up hills and through bushes. I am always the first to get bored. One of his favourite places to play is the lake near our house. He loves to dive under water in pursuit of his ball and doggy-paddle back to the bank. One particularly chilly day in October we were playing at the lake. I threw the ball and Vidar dived in as usual, oblivious to the cold. He swam around, his head poking out of the water, clenching the ball between his teeth. He'd drop it at my feet, shake the water off his coat, look at me, then look back at the ball waiting for me to throw it, tail wagging furiously.

Whenever I bent down to pick up the ball, he'd turn around and be ready to chase it, always one step ahead. Sometimes I'd tease him by pretending to throw it in the water, then hide it behind my back. Vidar would launch himself from the steep bank into the lake with an almighty splash, then doggy-paddle frantically in one direction, then the other, his mind trying to work out where it had gone. Confused, he would swim back to the lakeside and sit at my feet with an indignant "arf arf" as if to say, "I know you've got it. Just throw it."

After a while, I was starting to feel the autumnal chill through my down jacket and decided it was time to go home. So when Vidar returned, dropping the ball at my feet, I clicked his lead onto his collar. But at that point the ball rolled down the bank and back into the water. Vidar thought it was another game and launched himself into the lake, this time with me attached to the other end of the leash. I let go as I landed in a soggy tangle of reeds and mud. Vidar, meanwhile, had returned to the bank, ball in his mouth as if to say, "I got it. I got it."

It was a miserable walk home. My hair was matted with grass, my jeans clung damp and cold to my legs and my warm winter jacket was soaked through and filthy. Vidar, on the other hand, was looking especially proud, striding along with his tail in the air.

On the way we passed a man, who put £2.62

in my hand and said, "I hope your luck gets better, love."

I replied, "I'm not homeless, you know. He's just dragged me into the lake." I learnt my lesson that day; now I let Vidar hold onto his ball until we are safely away from the water.

Despite all his social blunders, when the two of us are alone together at home he is the most loveable softie you could ever imagine. When I'm watching TV he will creep across my lap and slowly worm his way up until his head is resting against my shoulder and I have no choice but to cuddle him like a baby. As I stroke the soft, silky blond fur on his belly, his eyes start narrowing and his tongue droops out to the side, the signal that he's totally relaxed. Whenever I stop stroking him, he'll open his eyes wide in disbelief as if to say, "How dare you?" and he'll tap my hand with his front paw until I start again. And then he'll fall asleep in my lap with my hands resting on his belly.

I never get tired of watching my sleepy boy getting ready for bed. I only have to say the words "Mammy's bed" and he lifts himself up from the rug or slinks down from the sofa, depending on where he's been sleeping, and lazily lollops down the hallway, his claws click-clacking on the wooden floor. By the time I turn the lights out and follow him to the bedroom, he's made himself comfortable in the centre of my double bed. He lies outstretched on his back, with his back legs slung to the left and his front paws sticking up in the air, eyes closed, shiny black lips closed tight and his greying muzzle gleaming in the dark. And that's where he stays; I have to find a space on the edge.

Sometimes during the night he'll wake me up with a growl. The first time it happened I woke with a start, thinking he'd heard an intruder. But when I looked at him, he was flat out on his back, his face twitching and his paws flapping as if he was running away from an imaginary enemy. Who knows what he dreams about – maybe he's trying to escape from Afghans torturing him or maybe he's running after another fur ball, but all I know is that it's the only time he will ever growl.

He has taught me so much about the breed and how to care for a non-working, working dog. We are learning together and loving every minute. When I first brought him home I didn't know what to expect, but now I have a fantastically loyal dog. He is twenty-six kilos of love.

Stargazers

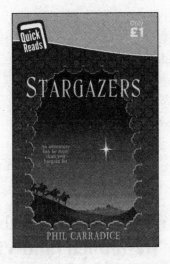

In a Middle-Eastern state, Yaniv plans to follow in his father's soldiering footsteps – he wants travel, adventure and respect. So the offer to escort some stargazers on a mysterious journey seems like a great opportunity. But his first mission isn't as straightforward as it is expected to be. Along the way Yaniv meets treachery, violence, danger and royalty, as well as a remarkable young girl. What are the stargazers really searching for? And who can he really trust?

For more information about
Angie McDonnell (and Vidar!)
and other **Accent Press** titles,
please visit:

www.accentpress.co.uk